Master Works

What distinguishes master works from other photographs? Attention to detail, planning, and craftsmanship. Visual literacy is a constant consideration, (knowing how to use the visual language, and then having something to say). Conceptualization is one of the things that make art, having a unique solution to the visual problem is another. Each one of these images is based on art concepts of contradiction, ambiguity, symbolism, aesthetics, or some combination of these concepts.

I use a 4X5 view camera, this is no more than a tool. The photographer should select the best equipment for the job at hand. Most of my pictures are still life photos that don't require mobility, so camera size is not important. The view camera forces you to slow down, therefore giving you more time to think and consider details. The cost of each sheet of film also makes you look for mistakes before they happen. Looking at the ground glass that is away from your eye to focus and compose is more like composing on a piece of paper. You think more about how the space is used. After the image is composed, I use a loupe (magnifying tool) to check focus on different areas of the ground glass. Exposure is critical. I use a spot meter to measure different areas of the image. The zone system is used to further control exposure. I still shoot film and make silver gelatin prints. I like to control the entire process, and love the look of a high quality silver gelatin print. These images are scanned directly from the original negative. They are an indication of the quality of the original prints.

Most of my photos are shot using artificial light; it is an essential element of the picture. When you control lighting, you control the mood of the photograph. Using continuous lighting most of the time allows you to see exactly how the light will look on the finished image. When elements of the picture move, I may use electronic flash. I try to keep lighting as simple as possible to preserve a natural appearance to the quality of the light.

Each photo is a work into itself. If it is part of a series the photo should stand on its own with its redeeming characteristics. The technique used to produce the work and concept are adapted to what works best for that image.

I don't always give names to photographs, but this one needed one. It's titled Genesis (SL49). I included the elements that are needed for the beginnings of life. Most life begins with an egg, water, and the sun. The parts of the picture are symbolic for all life.

The photo must be organized into a composition. The rule of thirds places the egg off center to aid in asymmetrical balance. The water spots create a pattern and the egg breaks the pattern. Many of the pictures I make use contradiction to entice the viewer. The elements here appear to defy the laws of physics, and create a contradiction.

The technique for this picture involved some complexity. There are three sheets of glass mounted in stands that are designed to hold them vertically. The glass sheet farthest from the camera had a piece of frosted acetate taped to it. An image of the sun setting on water was projected on to it. The second sheet of glass is mounted eight inches in front of that. I emptied the contents out of an egg to reduce its weight. This egg is taped to the second sheet of glass with double stick tape in a ball to help it conform to the shape of the egg. This second sheet is also mounted vertically on a table with an eight by ten inch hole in the table. The stand that holds the sheet of glass with the egg is mounted just back of the hole. A small spot light with a scrim to reduce the intensity of the light, and a snoot to concentrate the light only on the egg, was placed under the hole in the table. The egg was lit from the bottom. Care had to be taken to make sure light from the spotlight did not fall on the projected image washing it out. The last sheet of glass was closest to the camera. Water was sprayed on that sheet to increase the idea of the element of water, and create an additional patterned layer.

A small aperture of f64 was used to keep the two closest layers in focus, the egg and the water spots. The projected image on the last sheet is slightly soft. A long lens (215mm) was used to collapse perspective.

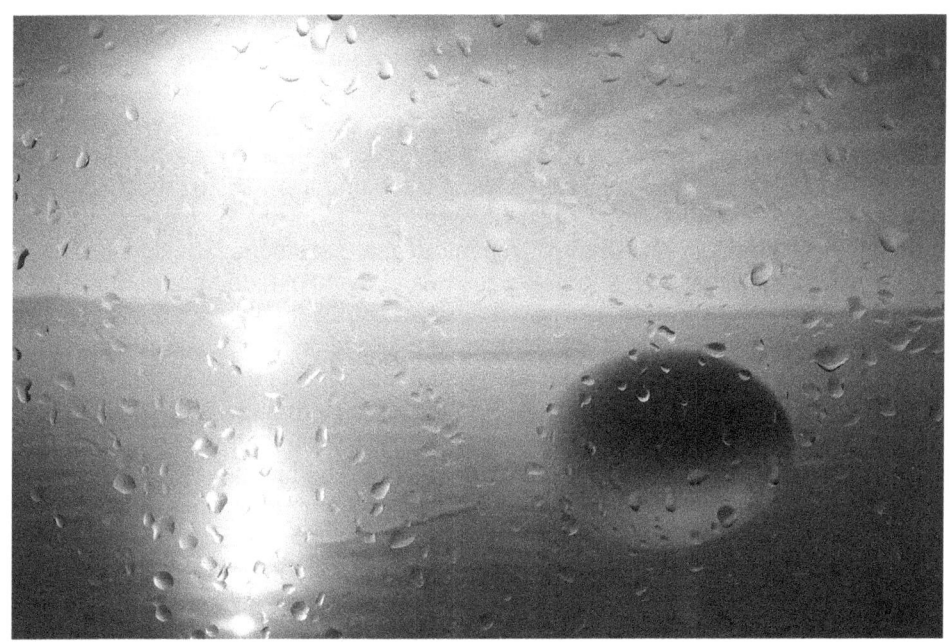

SL49

The concept for the Bubble series was based on the idea of their fragility and symmetry. Contradiction was the underlying art principle to keep the viewer engaged.

The composition uses the rule of thirds; contrast in tone was also a consideration. A psychological contradiction works to keep the viewers interest.

This image, like most of my work, took pre-planning. How would it look? And how would I do it? Pre-visualization must always come first. How will I have this image meet my aesthetic demands? First I used lighting to highlight the subject and create textured background that would contradict expectations. I designed the background by laminating a sheet of glass to a piece of clear plastic of the same size. The glass was covered with newspaper and struck in different places with a hammer. Because the glass was laminated to the plastic the shards of glass stayed in place. The glass was placed in a stand to hold it vertically. A sheet of frosted acetate was taped to the back. An electronic flash head with a snoot was placed at the rear of the glass. The flash was used because the short duration of the light would stop the movement of the bubble. The snoot concentrated the light at the center of the image creating tonal variation on the background. A hole was drill in the bottom of a plastic water bottle. The open end of the bottle was dipped in soapy water. Blowing in the drilled end of the bottle created the bubble at the open end. With practice, various sized bubbles were blown in front of the glass. When it floated into the right position, I knew I was ready to take the picture.

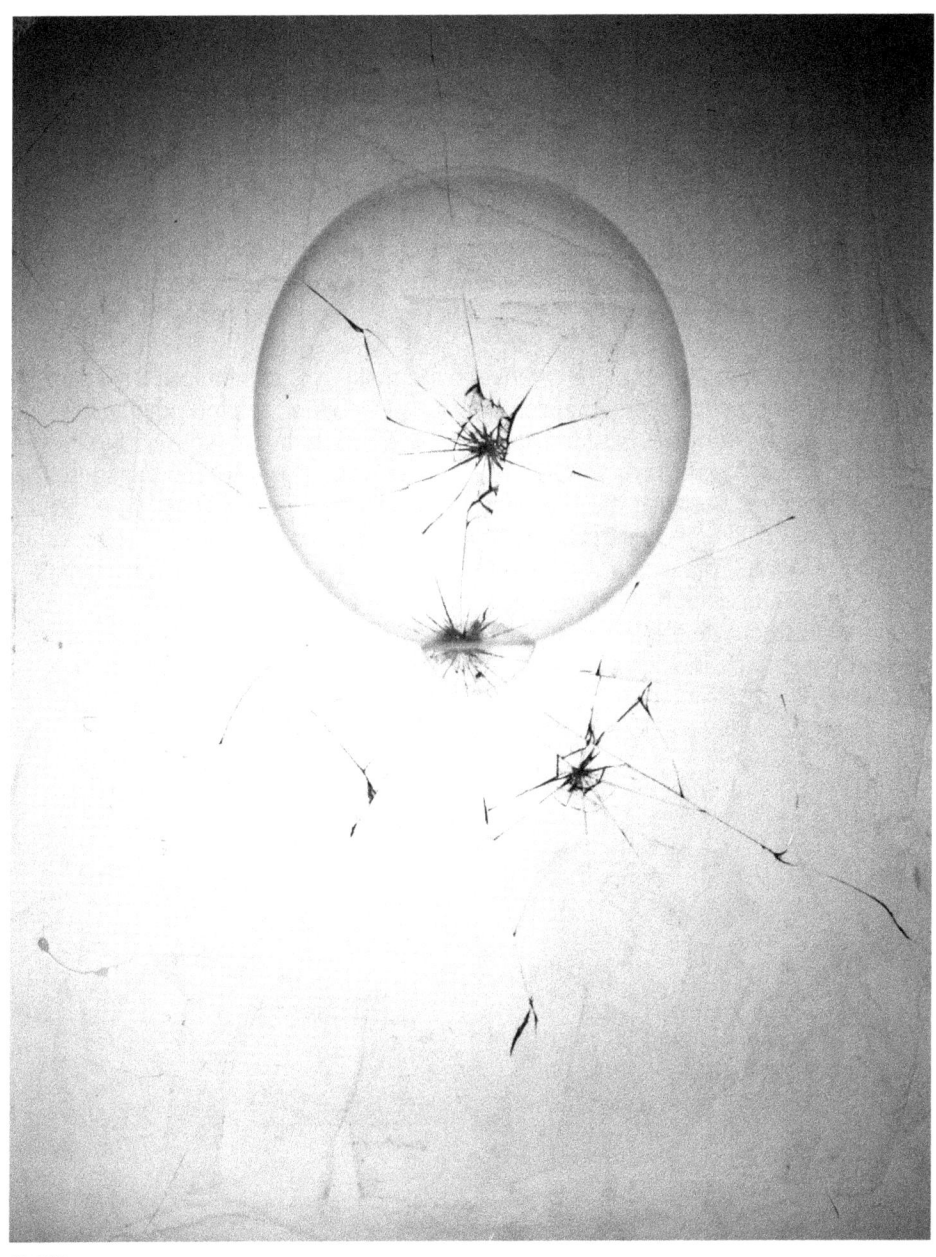

SL272

There was always something mysterious about looking through a keyhole. When we were children, it was always a thrill to look through into the next room. We are the sum of our experiences. This is important as an artist because those moments are often expressed through our art. This was a part of my childhood and was the driving idea for this photograph. The keyhole was the supportive element in the making of a photo that communicated an idea.

The compositional elements used in this photo were contrast in tone. I used lighting to create implied diagonal line to increase the feeling of drama. Deep shadows created contrast in tone to also increase the feeling of drama or mystery

Of course there was thought that went into the making of this image. Unlike some of my other photos the elements were there, I just needed to plan how to use them to express my idea. First the light coming through the keyhole had to be the brightest part of the picture. Your eye will almost always gravitate to the lightest area of a picture. Because the hole was so small it needed to almost glow. This bright opening also made you want to know what was on the other side; it was an invitation to look. This was a simple matter of putting a bare light bulb in front of the keyhole. The diagonal shaft of light accentuates the sense of drama. Diagonal lines create the felling of drama or action. A spot light with barn doors was used to shape the light. A reflector was used to keep the shadows from going black. The patina of the door was an important element in adding visual as well as psychological texture to the photo.

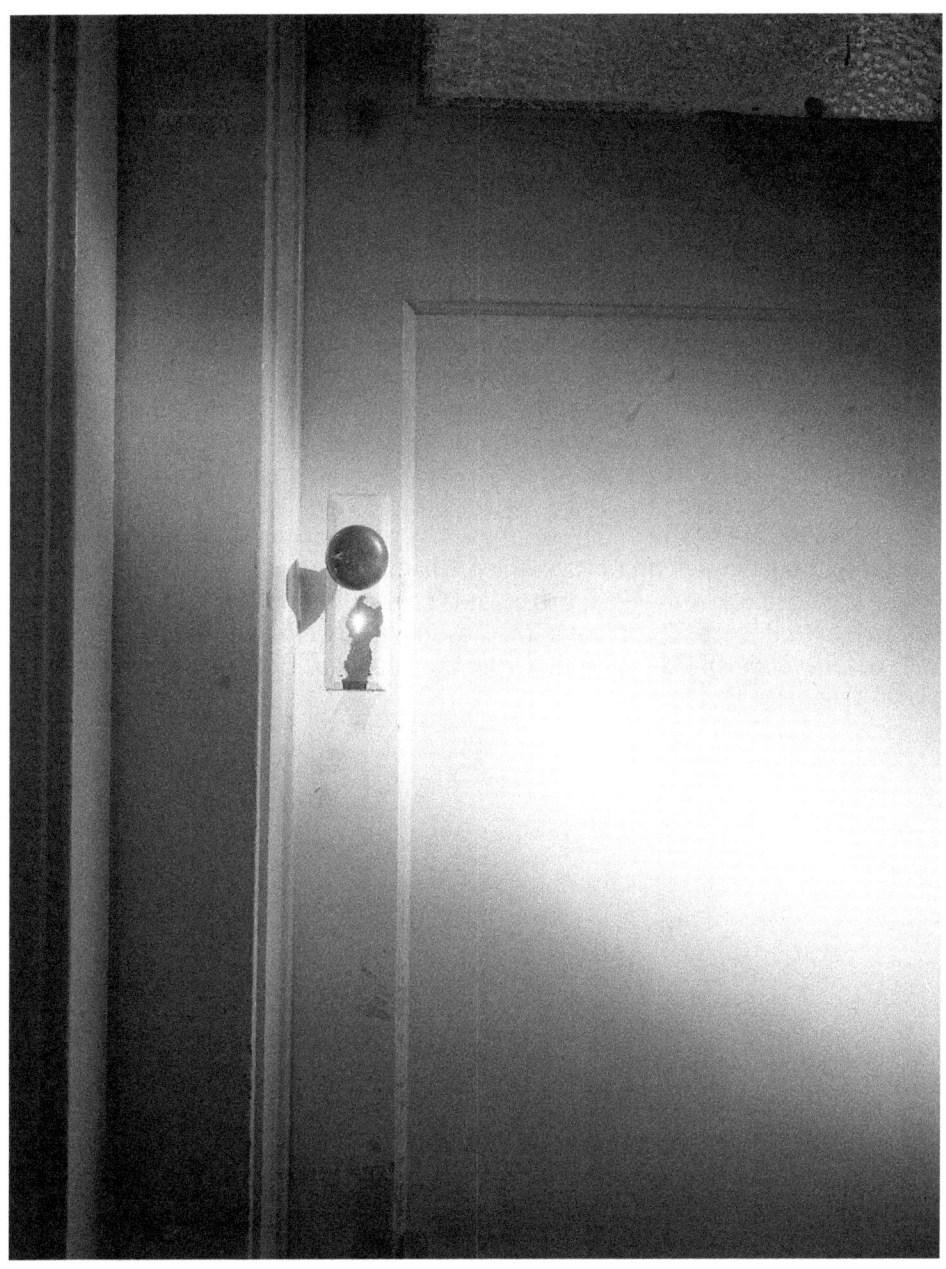

SL137

Glorification of nature is one of the long-standing themes in art. Many of us are familiar with the tradition of landscape photography from masters such as Ansel Adams, Edward Weston, and too many more to mention. I also shoot pictures following that practice but with a different approach. I shoot smaller, more intimate, and out of context pictures, following the theme of contradiction.

There were several photos using leaves in conjunction with water. One of my first was an image that gave the appearance of leaves by a frozen creek in the winter. I live in Los Angeles; we have no frozen creeks so I created it on a minor scale with rocks, sand, leaves and water that were placed in my freezer. It worked well, but had a common appearance. Art is developing a unique solution to a self-imposed visual problem. Simplicity is the essence of good design. How could I design a picture that gave the same feeling without being visually complex, and still be unique? The picture I made relies on pattern (visual rhythm) as a compositional element.

Several leaves are frozen in a block of ice in a large flat glass dish. The dish is placed on the table with an 8x10 opening. The dish is placed over the opening. A light is placed under the dish; this creates bottom lighting that accentuates the frozen leaves and ice. There are a few leaves added to the top, they are sprayed with water. A spot light shines light across their surface. This adds increased visual dimension and texture

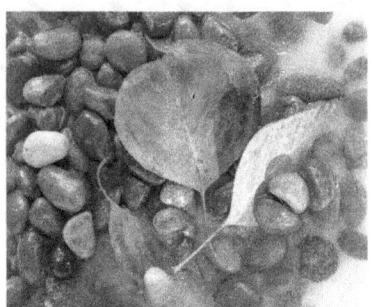

Leaves by a Frozen Creek. SL16

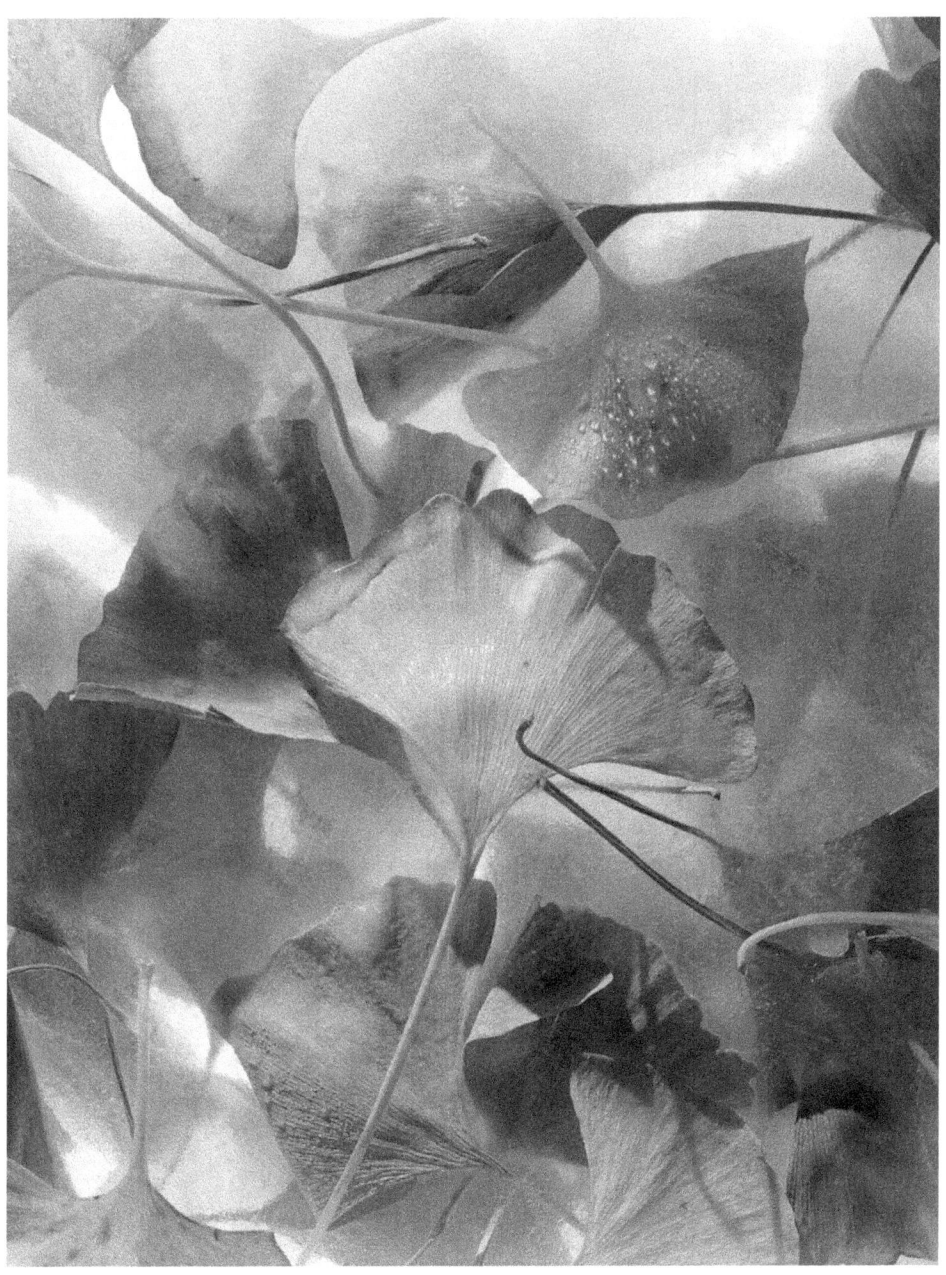

SL225b

The concept for this picture is based on religion; the stained glass window in the box is symbolic of that. The box tied up represents the entity that must decipher that religion for us. It is a mystery unless we have someone who interprets what we read or know about that religion. It is moving because it changes depending on who is telling us the stories.

No matter what we say with the symbols in a picture, it can always be enhanced by how we say it, that's the aesthetics. There are two important elements in this photo, the stained glass window in the box, and the second swinging box. They are connected to form one visual mass by the shadow created from the stained glass box. The shadow is deep in tone and diagonal to increased the feeling of drama. The window in the box is the lightest element, this draw your eye there first.

I cut a square opening into a sheet of white illustration board. I then made a box to fit the cut out opening. I made the box with tabs that folded out on to the back of the board. When mounted on the illustration board the tabs prevented stray light from coming in around the edges. The back open end of the box was covered with a sheet of frosted Mylar. The illustration board with its parts was mounted in a vertical position. The image of the stained glass was projected from the back. The set up was lit from the side by a small spotlight with barn doors to shape the light. A reflector was used opposite the light to keep the shadows from going too dark. The box on the string was moved about an inch to create the movement. The shutter was set at a slow speed ¼ second to show movement.

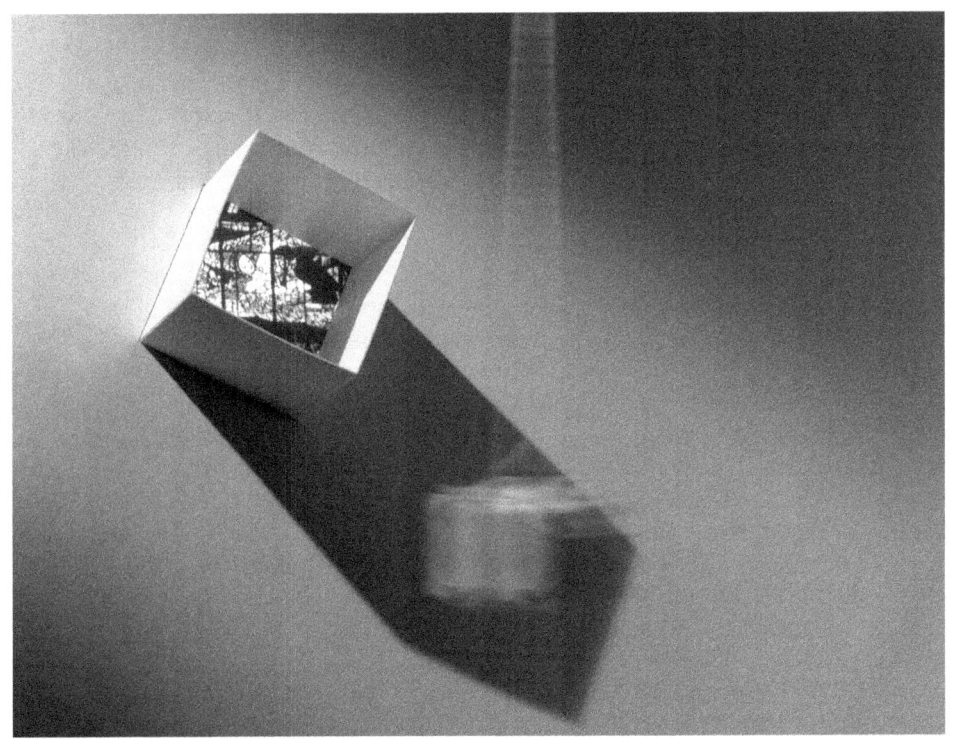

SL76

My series of feather pictures emanated from one idea. I found a deserted birds nest that had been in a hanging planter in my yard. I took it down, bought some quail eggs at the farmers market, put a few feathers around it, and had a picture. It was a good photo, but was it art? It was too graphic, plane and un-inspiring. My idea was to simplify the image and expand on the concept. There are several pictures in this series that expand on the original concept in different ways, using different techniques, this is but one. There are other photographs in this series that divert from the original idea and make no connection, but still use the feathers as a visual theme. The photo can ask the viewer to interpret, engage, or question the purpose, meaning, or concept of the artist.

The extreme contrast in tone between the subject and the background give you only one place to focus your attention, the egg and the feather. Both objects appear to be floating in space; this creates the appearance of a physical contradiction.

I used two wooden dowels about three feet long. I constructed a vertical stand, and painted the dowels and stand black. I drilled several holes in the face to the stand the same diameter as the dowels. I placed them in the stand so the feather and egg would be aligned. The contents of the egg were blown out and it was painted black. The shell was taped to the end of the lower dowel. The tip of the second dowel was sharpened to leave a 1/16-inch flat end. The vain in the feather was glued to that small flat area, and left to dry. The dowels were aligned again.

Lighting came from one spotlight directed from slightly rear and the right side of the egg. Small aluminum foil reflectors were used to lighten the shadows, and create separation from the background. Black velvet was hung behind the set up to absorb any light that might strike objects in the back.

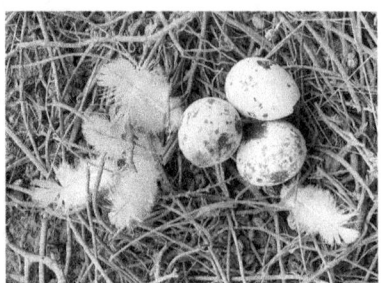

Birds Nest SL151

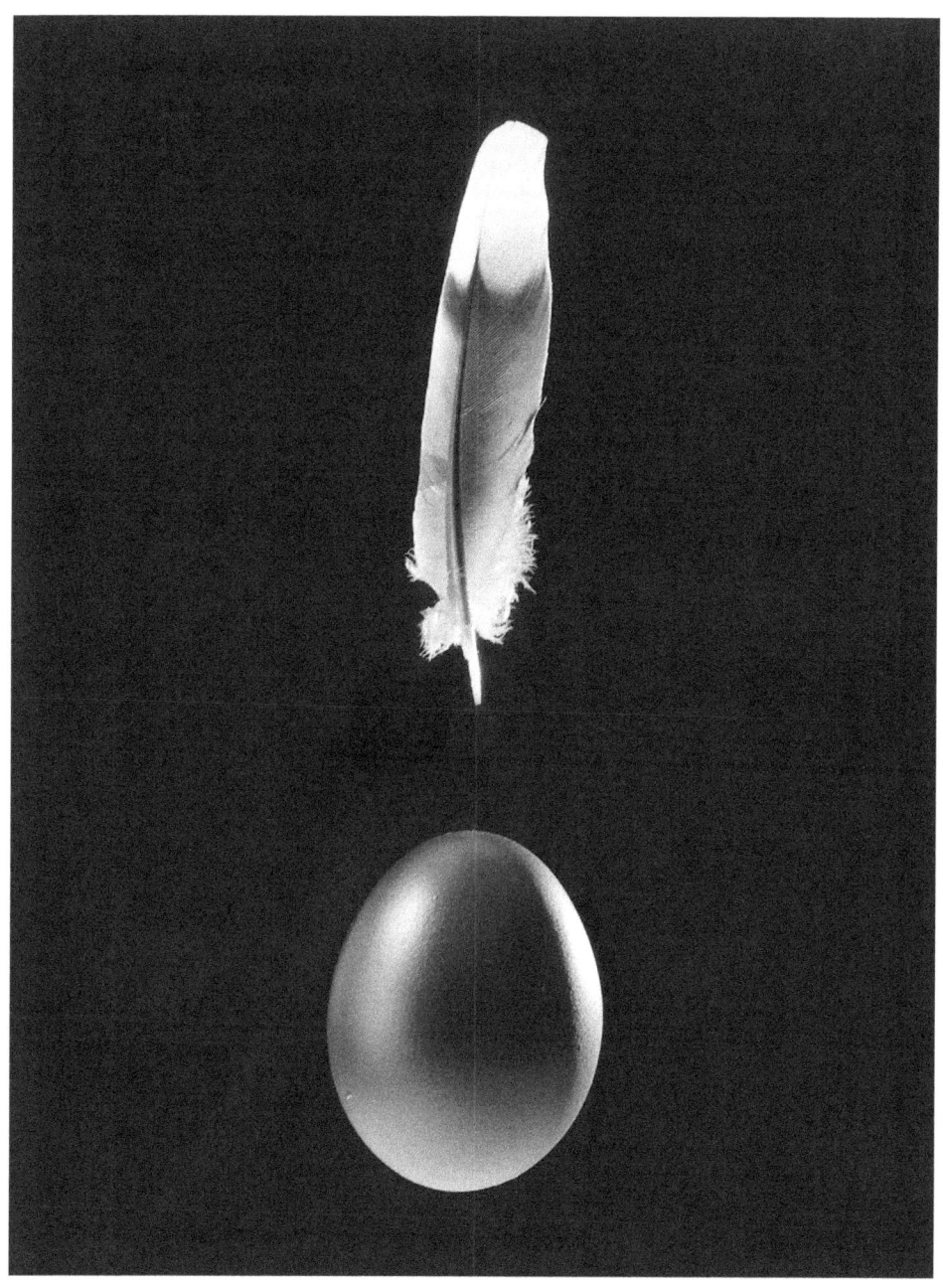

SL182

Photographers have learned to look, or remembered how to look. When we were young we had visual curiosity, we saw things in clouds, examined leaves, grass, bugs, and anything else we got our little hands on. As we matured most of us lost that curiosity. Some photographers still have it, and can find interest or beauty in many things. Most of the subjects I choose to photograph are the ordinary. My challenge is to make the ordinary extraordinary, to use my minds eye to see differently. Weeds are what we generally see as having little or no use; we work to get rid of them. They ruin our lawns, gardens, and farms. As an artist my efforts are to use my skills, sensibilities and minds eye, to raise even this weed to a place we call art.

I used the art theme of aesthetics to glorify nature. The image is a contradiction; the weed appears to float in air. The composition was based on contrast in tone and broken pattern.

The pattern is artificial; it is made of torn paper. This gives some tonal variation to the background. After I pulled the weed I washed the dirt from its roots. The weed was put between two sheets of glass. The paper was put behind another sheet of glass and put in a vertical position. A spotlight was placed at the rear to illuminate the picture.

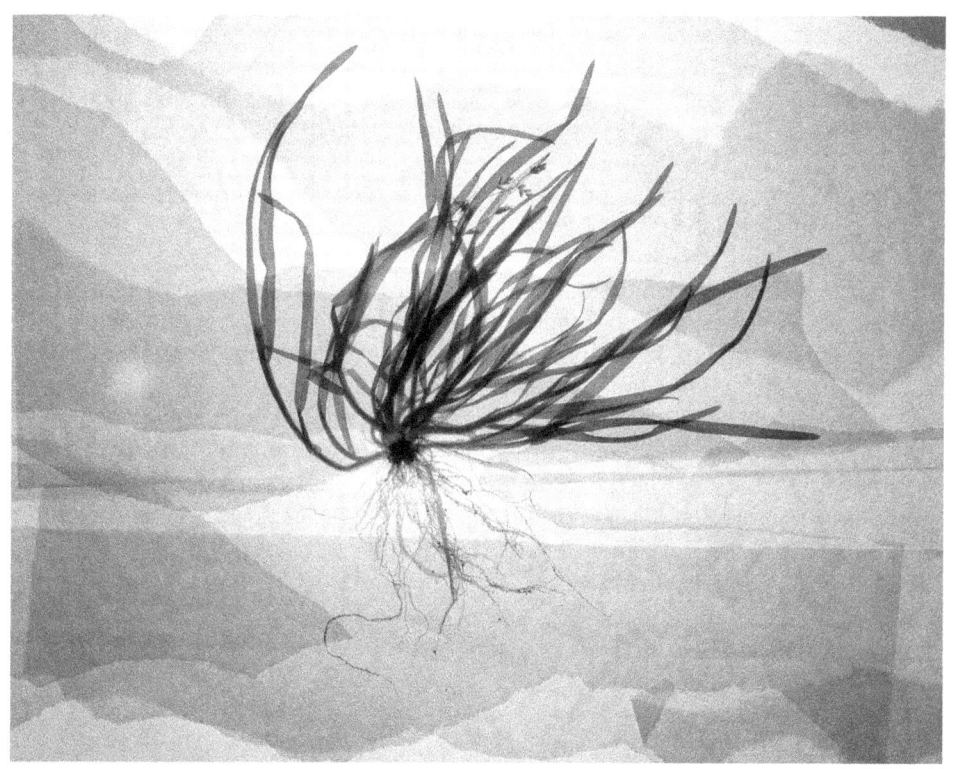

SL136d

It's not always what is said but often how it is said. Great speeches rarely have new ideas. It's all in the choice of words and delivery. Poetry is not so much based on content, but the beauty of the words and how they are used. If there is such a thing as visual literacy, and you strive to make work that is visually poetic, content may not be as important as other visual elements. This picture is little more than a hand full of feathers. The subject says little, but the concept of personal aesthetics is what contributes to the making of this photo.

This image uses contrast in tone and implied leading line to organize the picture. Physical contradiction also helps keep the viewer engaged.

Box parts were made from frosted mylar. The feathers were sorted by size. The small feathers were placed near the box and progressively larger ones were used as they went up. This helped give the illusion of the third dimension. The feathers and mylar were sandwiched between two sheets of glass. They were put in the vertical position. Frosted mylar was taped to the back of the assembly. A slide of sky was selected from my archive; I selected one that had a light area in the middle. Your eye will go to the brightest area of a picture. The image from the slide was projected and the picture made

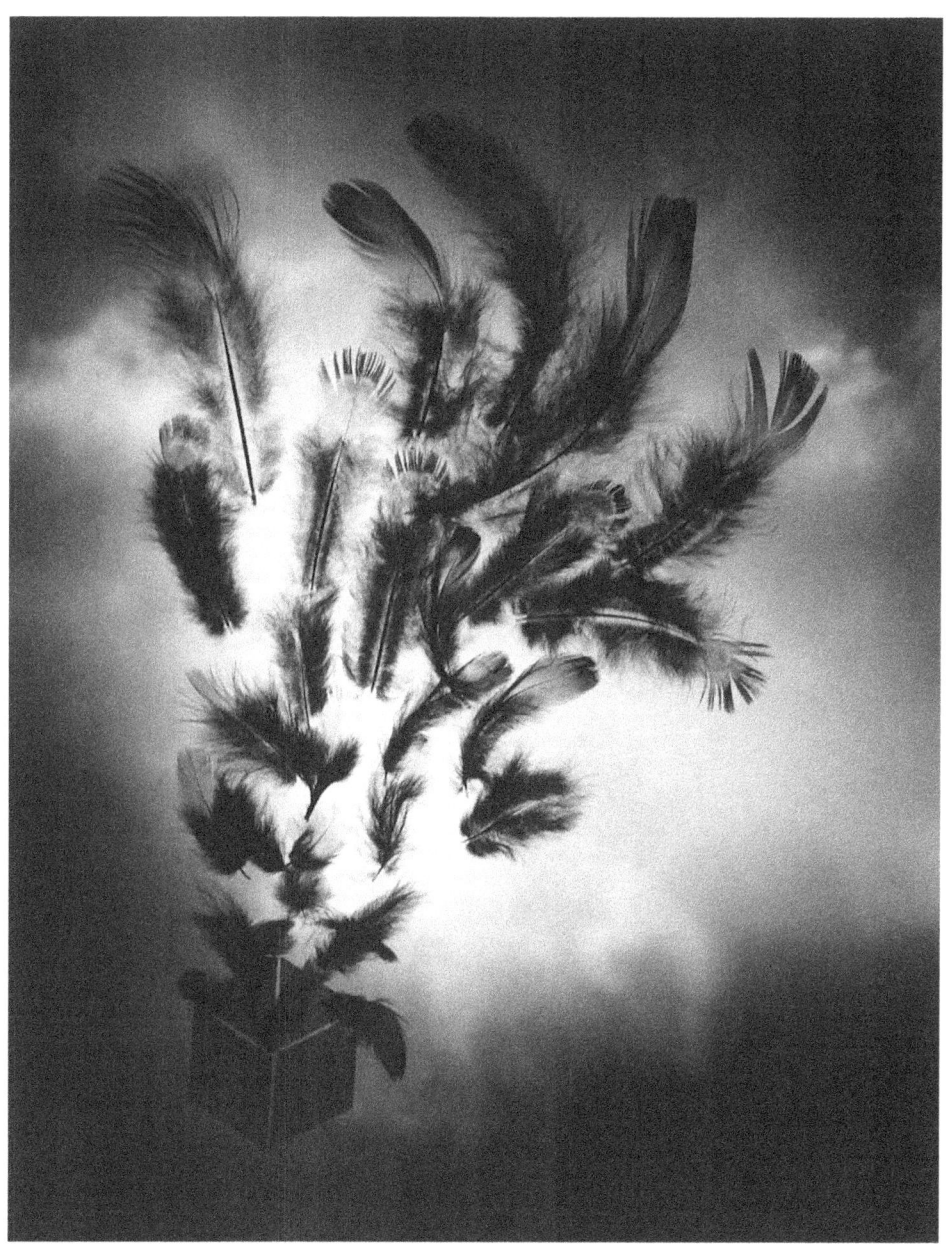

SL303

We have containers and wrapping for everything. We are at the point where our planet is polluted by the packaging. When I see individual pieces of fruit wrapped, I ask why? What's next? Do we package the individual leaves on the trees, or the plants in the earth. The idea that stores in some cities will not give out free bags is a start. This picture is a nod to our desire to package and market everything, even what's free. For this picture it's important that the fern behind the bag, is the same as the fern in the bag. They were also photographed the same way.

Contrast in tone helps keep your eye on the fern against its light background. There are tonal variations to add interest and send your eye to the lighter area.

A brown paper bag was taken apart and used as a pattern for a bag made of Mylar. Frosted mylar was taped to a sheet of glass. This is mounted in a vertical position. Fern was taped to the glass on the edges out of the cameras view. Where the fern was in contact with the glass, it appears sharp. The focus becomes softer for the parts that were not in contact the glass. The bag is attached to the glass with double stick tape. Fern is added to the bag. The lighting is a single spotlight behind the setup.

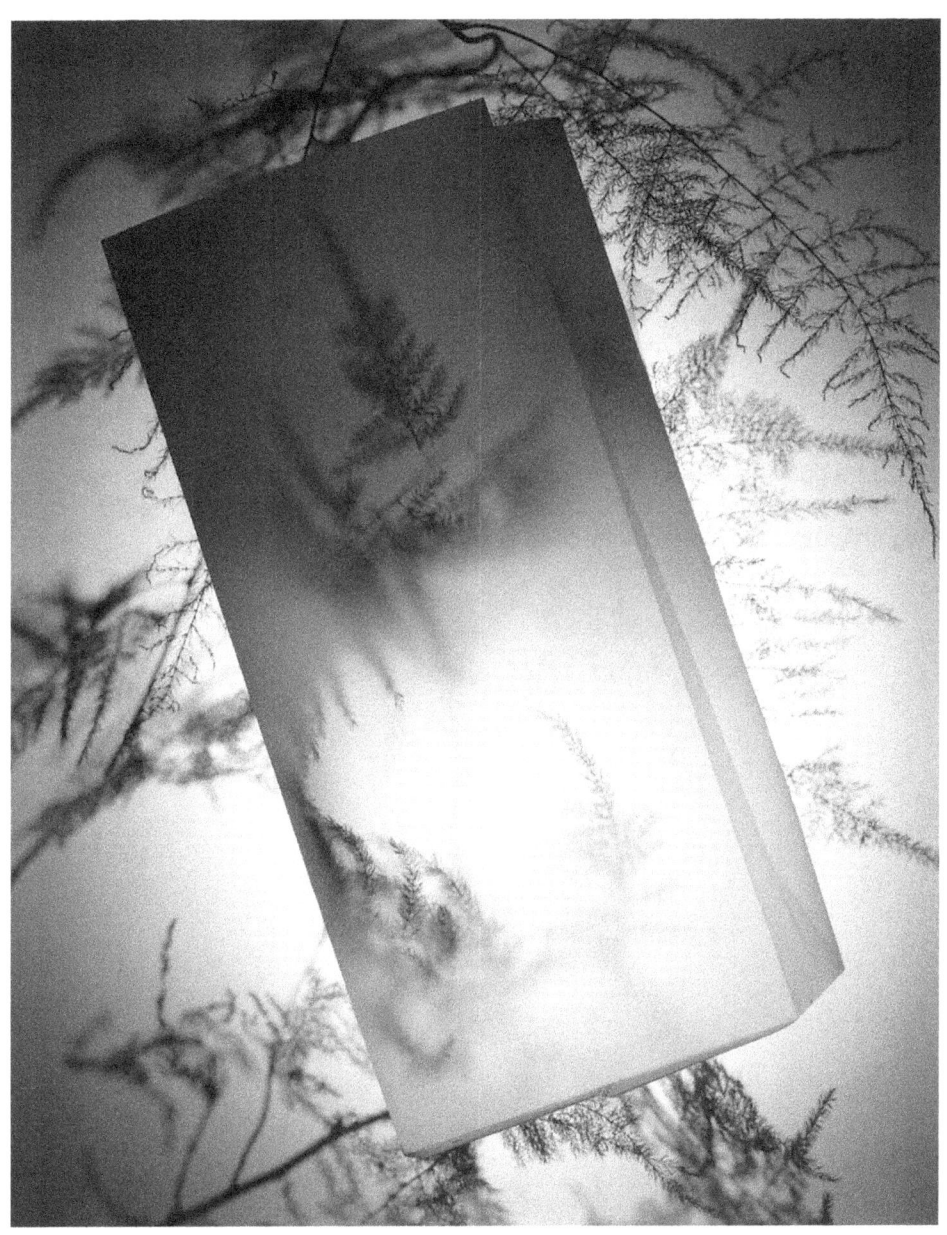

SL283

Time is running out. We have confined wild life to these boxes we call national parks. Many species are on the brink of extinction because we have boxed them out of areas that we "need". We must find solutions to keep the planet diverse and functional. When I started thinking about this, I ask myself, how can I express this idea in a single picture? I think this picture expresses my concept.

Contrast in tone helps make the picture stark and direct. The symbolism of the stopwatch and lion in the box, help communicate the idea.

The box with the lion in it had no bottom. This was glued to an illustration board with a hole cut in it that matched the size of the container. Frosted acetate was added to the bottom. I pulled a slide of a roaring lion from my archives and projected it onto the acetate bottom of the box. Other boxes were made and glued into place. The stopwatch was hung. A small slit of light from a spotlight with barn doors was the only other light source. It was positioned in the upper right corner. The light from the spot skimmed across the surface to create deep long shadows and increase the feeling of drama.

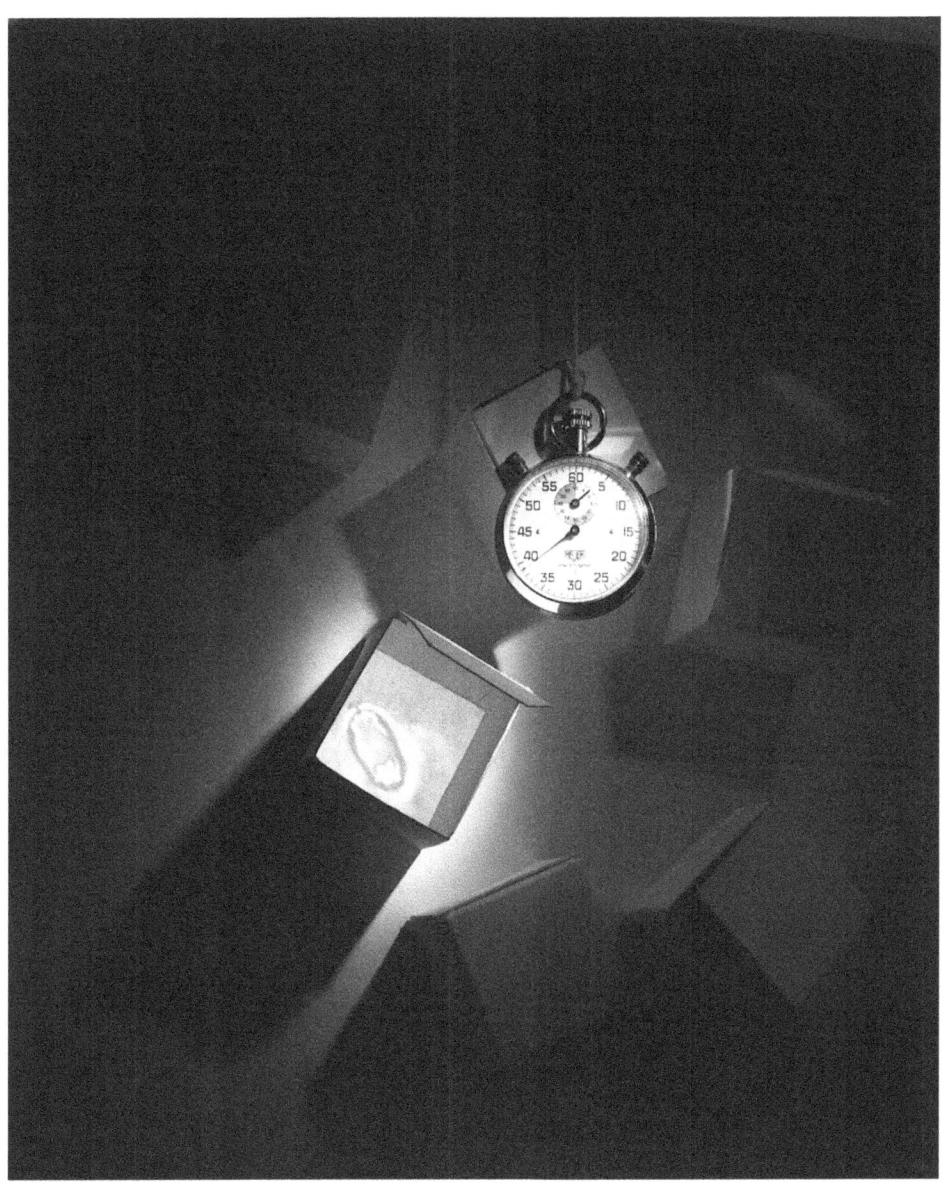

SL230c

Clean simple and to the point, elegant and understated. That's the foundation of the art I try to create. I would hope that these bubbles achieve that goal. I think the photographer must be inquisitive, and be a visual explorer. You must look at everything from different angles, explore the quality of the light, and manipulate backgrounds. It is important to play with different exposures, and shutter and aperture combinations. Above all, as much as time will allow, stop and contemplate. Art requires you to think, why am I making this image, and how should I make this photo?

Contrast in tone and unique angle of view or the compositional elements that help to organize this image. Aesthetics is the reason for the photo. Find beauty in the most simple of things.

Black velvet was hung above, and draped over a table; this cloth was used as the background. The bubbles are on a mirror. The edges of the mirrors are concealed with black tape. Lighting was simple. A round white scrim with a light behind it was used as the only light source. I had to work quickly because bubbles would break and I blew new ones during the process. Exposure was determined by reading the bright reflection in the bubble with a spot type light meter. I used the zone system for final exposure calculation.

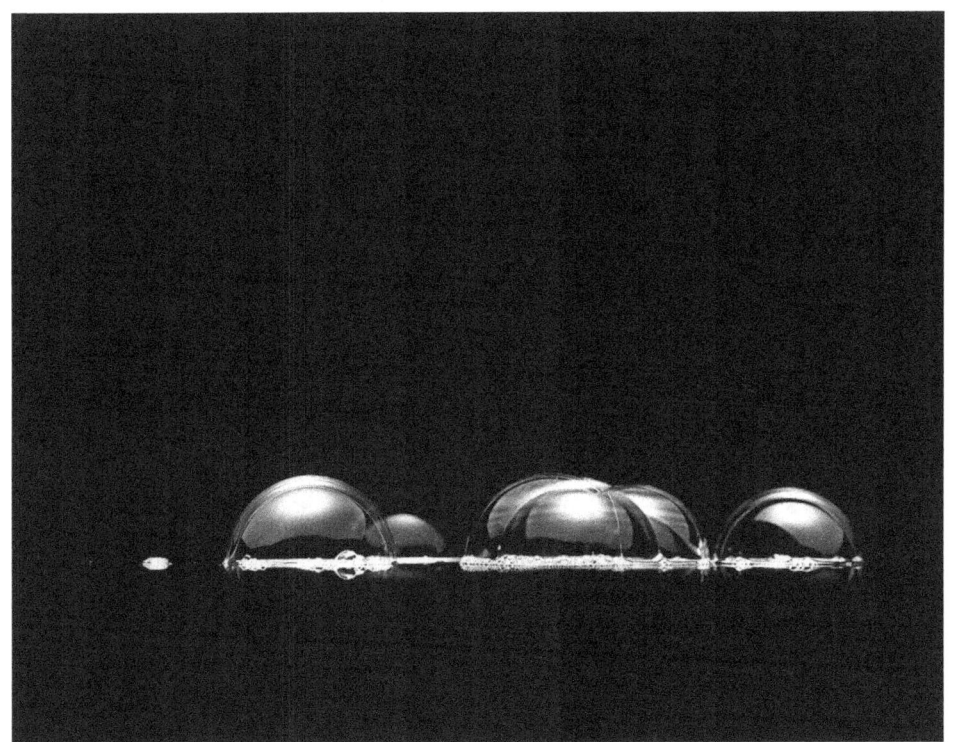

SL264

I believe you should always be true to the media you are using. Each way of producing art has its unique characteristics. Photography has the ability to show, or stop the effects of motion. The photo is also very graphic. No matter the subject or method, I try to always retain the graphic nature of the image. The picture should always look like a photograph, not something else. When I have the opportunity to introduce this mediums unique ability to effect movement I will incorporate that into the image. The picture should not be lost to methodology. How you do it should never override content. Don't do the trick for the sake of the trick, but to enhance the subject in some way

This photo is composed using contrast in tone and the rule of thirds. There is a physical contradiction used to get the viewers attention

The upside down feathers are hanging from fishing line. Fanning them with a piece of cardboard creates the movement. A slow shutter was used to show the blurred moving feathers. The single still feather is glued to a wooden dowel. The dowel is inserted into a black stand. The area behind the feathers is draped with black velvet. The light comes from a single spotlight on the left. Barn doors are used on the spotlight to keep light from striking the background.

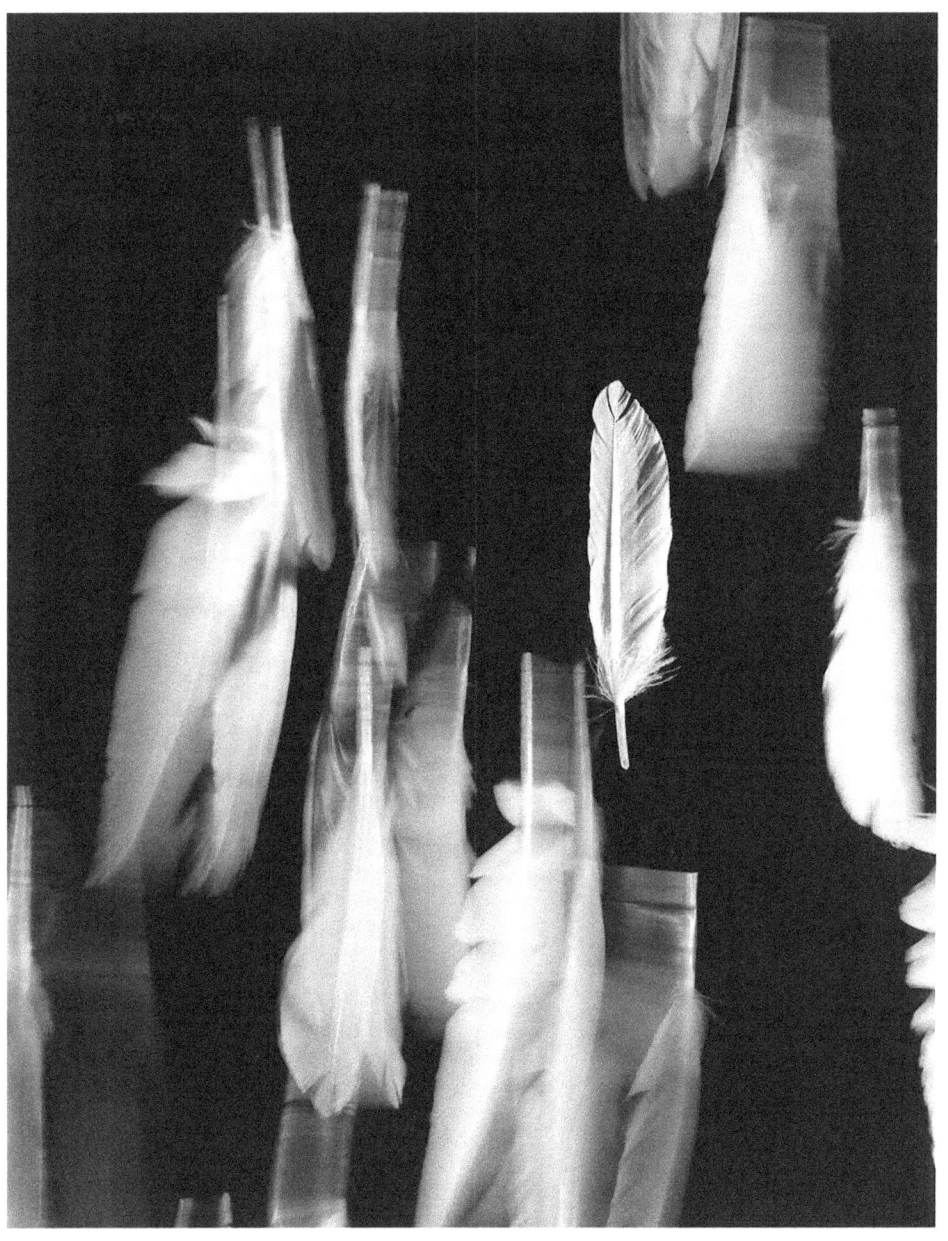

SL80

Contact Information

Gregory Talley

(323) 732-6058

geetalley46@hotmail.com

gregorytalleyartphotography.com

gregorytalley.blobspot.com